TMG BOOK SERIES PRESENTS

How To Get Great Dating Outcomes In A Modern World

Part I

By
Glenn Sandifer II

Copyright © 2025 by Glenn Sandifer II

All rights reserved. No part of this book may be reproduced in any form or by any electronic or mechanical means, including information storage and retrieval systems, without permission in writing from the publisher, except by a reviewer who may quote brief passages in a review.

Published By
Bellevue Publishers

www.BellevuePublishers.com

CONTENTS

Chapter 1 9
   What Is The Modern Ground? 9
   What Does Success Look Like? 13
   The Leader And The Helper 14
   Success Takes A Shot 15
   How Did We Get Here? 17
   I Don't Owe Anyone Anything 18
   Key Takeaway 19

Chapter 2 20
   Boys To High-Value Men 20
   Boys Will Be Boys 22
   I Need A Hot Boy 24
   He's Just Some Guy I Know 25
   They Male It In 27
   Male Mentality, Not Mamba 28
   Calling All The Real Men 29
   Who Are You Fighting For? 32
   Key Takeaway 36

Chapter 3 37
   Girls To High-Value Women 37
   Baby Girl – She Ain't Ready 38

Feelings Over Facts.. 39

What's Your Fantasy?.. 40

Friends, How Many of Us Have Them?.................................... 41

She's A Hot Girl, Living For The City 42

Wait, You Just Said... 43

Chaos Theory... 44

    Gal Pal... 46

    Don't Do It Tim!..47

Femme Fatale –.. 49

    Too Many In Here.. 49

    I Have Become Numb To All This...................................... 50

    A Negative Nancy (Karen).. 51

All Together Now.. 52

I AM WOMAN 53

Who's That Pokémon? Or What Do You................................. 58

    Boss Chick..59

    I'M A D..a..Diva. – Divas 60

Precious And Valuable – High Value Women........................ 62

    SMV – Why High-Value Women Win 64

    I GOT THESE DEGREES! 65

Key Takeaway.. 66

CLOSING STATEMENTS..68

INTRODUCTION TO PART I

I am sure you have purchased other relationship books. You have been searching for the answer to that burning question: Why aren't I married? While other books give you all the external reasons and factors that may be causing you not to achieve the outcome you want, this book is different. In fact, let me warn you that you may not like what I have to say. The thing that sets this book apart from the dime-a-dozen other books out there is that I will be real with you. Within these pages, I will help you identify why the problem is not out there, waiting for you to pull back the covers and suddenly find your soulmate. I will enlighten you to the harsh reality that you are the one holding yourself back from finding true happiness in a relationship.

In society today, most women have more money, access, influence, and responsibility than at any time in history. With that, women universally have expressed dissatisfaction with relationship outcomes. Translation: Women are not achieving the relationship outcomes they have dreamed of, those that were promised if they achieved more success with education and in their professions. They believe the strategies that allowed them to achieve this success will allow them to achieve success in relationships. THEY WILL NOT.

In society today, most men have more access to information than at any time in history. This access leads to the perception of choice. With that, men, universally, have expressed dissatisfaction with the dating pool of available women. Translation: Men are not achieving the relationship outcomes they have desired. THEY WILL NOT.

Instead, men and women need to look within themselves to understand how they can change the course of their existing relationships or find the true love that is waiting for them. How? Well, I cannot share that with you *now*, can I? No, that would be like giving away the ending of a movie before it has even begun. But spoiler alert: It Will Take Doing The Work!

This book speaks to the corporate executive, aspiring executive, solo-prenuer, entrepreneur, or high-earning individual struggling with the balance of managing successful relationships while finding sustained success in their professional careers.

With the help of this book, you will successfully identify why your relationship outcomes are: **1)** your fault, **2)** under your control, **3)** and your responsibility to fix. The world does not owe you or me understanding and expecting it from your partner solely will lead to disappointment. Your business or company pays you for the value you add to the business; your relationship does not. Your relationship is about giving yourself to another person to identify and meet their needs. Yet, you understand this with your business but fail at this in your relationship. A successful outcome with this book will be a change in mindset around romantic relationships and a pivot to selfless relationships to get the outcome you desire. Our upcoming sequel will outline the phase AFTER finding *The Modern Ground*.

Chapter 1

What Is The Modern Ground?

It is common to hear both men and women lament their relationship status, especially as social media encourages people

To share this status for the world to see. Men and women are not achieving the relationship outcomes they desire. Sadly, we see a 50 percent divorce rate across the country and even higher percentages in communities of Faith and Color. This begs the question: What led to these outcomes?

In this book, let's begin with the "Relationship Equation." Man + Woman = Couple

I am only qualified to discuss this scenario.

There was a recent study conducted by Randy Olson. The data is from the CDC NCHS. The link will be provided at the end of the book; however, the chart provided gives you a look at some key milestones and how they relate to marriage and divorce.

- The marriage rate peaked shortly after the end of World War II with 16.2 marriages per 1,000 people in 1946. Olson noted there was an increase in marriage rates at the start of both

    World War I (1917) and WWII (1942) and at the conclusion of both wars in 1918 and 1945.

- Just as the marriage rate increased following WWII, the biggest spike in divorce rates occurred immediately following the war, reaching 4.3 divorces or annulments per 1,000 people in 1946 – more than double the rate at the start of the decade. The divorce rate then quickly dipped back to near pre-war levels during the 1950s.

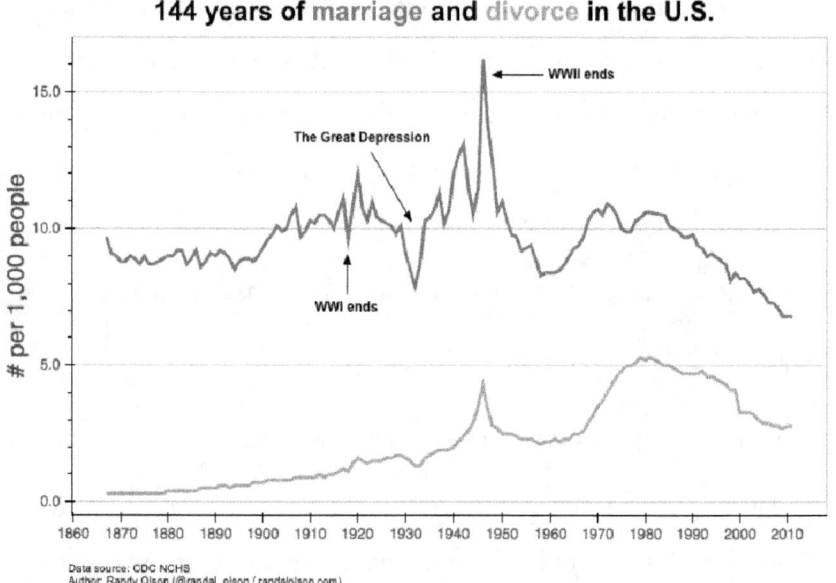

- Olson notes that, after taking population into account, marriage rates are the lowest they've ever been in recorded U.S. history.

How did we get here? The peak reflects the height of the Baby Boom, from which we get the term Baby Boomers (children born between 1945-1964). These children were typically born into a heterosexual, two-parent home. The average median income was equivalent to around $50,000 in 2019. The father was the breadwinner of the family and fit the traditional role we associate with men. The mother was the homemaker of the family and fit the traditional role we associate with women.

- The most notable drop in marriage rates occurred during the Great Depression as the rate went from 10.1 marriages per 1,000 people in 1929 to 7.9 in 1932.

- The divorce rate steadily increased after 1962, reaching a peak of 5.3 divorces or annulments per 1,000 people in 1979 and 1981. Since then, the rate has steadily declined. There was a significant drop – from 4.1 to 3.3 – between 1999 and 2000.

- In 2009, the divorce rate hit its lowest mark since 1968 with 2.7 divorces or annulments per 1,000 people.

- The marriage rate hit its lowest mark in 2010 at 6.8.

Something happened around 1964. Our new president announced the creation of one of the greatest Social Service

Programs in the history of the United States: The Great Society. The **Great Society** was a set of domestic programs in the United States launched by Democratic President Lyndon B. Johnson in 1964–65. The main goal was the total elimination of poverty and racial injustice. This great initiative led to a substantial increase in government spending on domestic/social programs. Programs that resulted from this effort were: The National Endowments for the Arts and Humanities, Public Broadcasting, Welfare, Medicare, Medicaid, Privacy laws, Education initiatives, Social Security Expansion, the Expansion of Public Housing Grants, Food Stamps Programs, and Unemployment Insurance.

As you can imagine, families began to lose value as more women chose to rely on Social Programs and less on the Natural Order. This order is that men provide, women nest, and children grow and develop.

So, men and women now find themselves in a precarious position where their desires, expectations, and outcomes do not align. As professional careers and success have taken precedence over the viability of relationships, both members of the species look

For guidance on managing relationships and careers or, in other words, *The Modern Ground*.

What Does Success Look Like?

Partners seeking partners seems to be the norm for the average person in today's society. Being average is OKAY! But when it comes to relationships, we seem to be failing in dating and marriage outcomes at an alarming rate. In reality, we are failing to reach The Modern Ground with one another. If we look at women, women have more money, more access, more opportunity than at any time in history, which has changed how they approach dating and their needs. Men feel they're getting left behind from a leadership standpoint in relationships because of that change. An unfortunate statistic reveals that only one in two women will marry at any point in their lifetime. This is a far cry from the average of 65 percent of women who married in the 1950s. Further to this extremely low marriage rate, on average, 60 percent of those married women ultimately file for divorce when they decide to leave.

When I decided to write this book, I wanted to understand the root of these relationship failures and help relationship-seekers get back to The Modern Ground. In The Modern Ground, both men and women can be truly fulfilled. In short, I believe The Modern Ground can be met by just having an honest discussion about where we are and how we got here and then getting everyone on the same page. Relationships as a whole have the purpose of providing a sense of comfort, companionship, connectivity, and community. We often find it difficult for those who don't have that relationship to have the overall level of success they're looking for. Sure, people earn more money, travel the world, and drive fancy cars, but are they fulfilled? Are you fulfilled? Success is about more than what you have in the bank account or how many trips you have taken. It is about what you contribute to society, your friends, family, and ultimately, the life of another person. How you grow and develop

Together will be key in everything you do. Success is nothing without friends and family to share your success. Life is better when you have *one* person with whom you can share your entire story!

The Leader And The Helper

Now, I know these two words may be triggering for some, and you may want to throw this book at my head. But let's look at the definitions of each of them before we discuss how they relate to relationships in which the husband is to be the leader and the woman the helper. According to Dictionary.com, a leader is a person who leads or commands a group, organization, or country, the principal player in any group. In other words, a leader understands their role, and their function is the support of an entire people, family, community, city, state, or country. A leader has a selfless motive when identifying themselves as a leader. You can develop yourself into a leader, but it takes time, and leaders have to be selfless. People don't lead just to lead. Leaders need someone to help them, as they cannot be expected to do it alone. Have you ever tried to be the leader of something but had no one to support you? Ultimately, you will fail without the assistance of those whose role it is to help.

A helper is defined as someone who provides assistance and support. Their focus is coming up under the authority of a leader and executing the strategy of that leader. We find these roles defined in the Bible and nature, and when everyone stays within their leadership role or in their helper role, things move smoothly. But, when things get out of order, roles are confused or misinterpreted, a misalignment occurs, and arguments ensue. When this happens, there are hurt feelings, missed opportunities, and long-term consequences in any organization. In a relationship, we see people hurt feelings and derail the entire relationship, due to the misunderstanding of these roles.

That is where we see most struggles that individuals face when trying to engage in a relationship with the opposite sex. Who is the leader? Whose role is it to be the helper? We have diverged from these functions, with so many men being raised by strong, single women over the last few decades. Men no longer know what it means to lead and to have the responsibilities of a leader, such as providing and protecting. Women have taken on these tasks and are unwilling to relinquish control or become the helper. Generations of young people have been raised to believe partnerships are the way to a healthy, successful marriage or relationship. Therefore, moving away from the roles of leaders and helpers, they find themselves out of alignment.

Success Takes A Shot

Let's talk a little bit about what the word *success* looks like when it comes to relationships. Success for a heterosexual couple is marriage with children. I'm not even going to say a happy marriage because marriage is really about duty, which no one wants to talk about. It should be a thriving marriage and relationship. I know duty is another one of those words that will cause the hair on the back of your neck to rise and your skin to crawl. No one wants to think of marriage as a duty, but that is exactly what it is: commitment, honor, respect, and love. These are all tasks or actions that each person is required to perform. We know we have domestic duties, childcare duties, employment duties, military duties, religious duties. But, when it comes to marriage, the word duty sparks an outpouring of upset, disgust, and revulsion like no other. Why?

I'll say it this way. We have been trained indirectly in the West to think marriage is about a feeling, while it has always been about duty in every other region. When a man signs up to be a husband, in most instances, he should know that his job is not to be served but

To serve. His duty as a husband is to encircle the entire family to protect it. People are getting married because they want a wedding, a honeymoon, and, ultimately, a partnership. They don't understand the responsibility and the duty related to marriage.

Men are responsible for being the protector, the provider, the priest, and the prophet in their homes. As the leader in my home, I need to be the one to create an atmosphere that allows the children to thrive and my wife to feel protected and secure. That is my duty. Even when she makes me mad, I'm not ready to divorce her because I have a duty that trumps feelings. Yet, we are now a society in which feelings trump duty.

How Did We Get Here?

My grandfather had a nice, simple life. Not a life most modern men want today, but it was consistent across most communities in the United States at that time. Most modern men are afraid of this simple truth: I have no idea how to lead the way my grandfather or great grandfather did! Most modern women rebel against the idea of a traditional marriage. In part due to this statement, but also due to circumstance, they have the communicated traumas of their great grandmothers and grandmothers as their guiding light, even though these women were married at a greater rate and stayed married until the death of their spouse, which both my grandmothers did. It was because these women of the Silent Generation/Traditionalists understood their stated and assigned roles: Serve and help. Their duty was clear and shared with their family and friend groups: support our husbands, raise the kids, and keep a home as a peaceful place. Modern women will hear this and echo, "You want to send me back to the fifties?" No one wants to send anyone anywhere. But the fear that's associated with it is a lack of connection of duty. It is also associated with a lack of true examples. Most women that have been in successful marriages are

not honest with single modern women about what it takes to make it work. "I got mine; you get yours," is the prevailing theme.

We also have an entire generation of men and women who never lived in a house with a male figure! How do you ask someone to vacuum if they have never seen a vacuum cleaner? Yes, there is food on the floor, and we want it up. Since it's carpet, it takes a special tool to remove the food. But we then tell you to use this device you have never seen. That is the equivalent to what we asked our women; get married to a man. Something you have never seen! And oh, by the way, make it work. They don't know what to do. For men, get married to a woman and support her. Provide for her and protect her! And you need to do it with a smile! Again, how in the hell are they going to vacuum if you give them a dustpan and broken broom with no handle?

I Don't Owe Anyone Anything

The Modern Ground begins with both parties operating in good faith. This means coming to the table with a clear understanding of what they value and what they can provide a mate. If that mate is a partner, what you provide is different from what a leader does. Not all partners will stay partners. At some point, they can transition to helper or leader. It is my opinion and proven through nature that men lead and women help. When this harmony is met, great things happen for our communities, nation, and society. If men and women will enter a relationship with the goal of knowing and accepting these roles and accepting that marriage is about duty from both parties, setting the *"you"* aside, marriages would remain intact, and families would thrive. It is possible to achieve the relationship outcome you desire if you can change your mindset and way of thinking.

In the next chapters, we will look at the various types of men and women and help you to identify what type of mate you currently are, what type of man/woman you qualify for, and then ultimately, how to grow and develop into the position that is most attractive to a mate best suited for you.

Key Takeaway

Don't look for a partner if you want a helper. Don't look for a partner if you want a leader. If you are looking for either, make sure you understand what both the Helper and Leader (exceptional/rare) are and what they are seeking.

Chapter 2

Boys To High-Value Men

You are a man or want a man. That is my guess because, otherwise, based on the title and introduction, you would not still be here. But I want to recalibrate your understanding of the word *man*.

There is a difference in the male species, with various types of men each wondering why they can't find a mate. Both men and women don't realize they fall into these categories that may hold them back from finding true love. Upbringing, expectations, financial status, and desires impact the relationship outcomes they achieve. In the following pages, we will talk about each of the six types of men, their characteristics, and therefore, the expectations of each.

Men, know that no matter which category you find yourself in, you can make a change and achieve the relationship outcome you desire if, in fact, you *want* to make a change in your life. I will tell you how, so keep reading. These categories of men, of course, correspond to various categories in which women fall as well, the

misalignment of which causes a breakdown in communication and disconnect in relationships.

There are six types of men in the dating environment: High-Value Men (Men of Value, Productive Men), Men (White Collar, Blue Collar or Modern), Males, Guys or Dudes, Hot Boys, City Boys or FCUK Boys, and Boys. So, when you find yourself in conflict, remember there are six different types of men. Of course, if you are a woman asking the question, "How will I know which category a man falls into?" Ladies, the truth is a tough one: you won't know until it is too late. On the other hand, a man may not realize which of these categories he is in until he tries repeatedly and fails to find a relationship that suits him. We will get to how to work through the type of man you want to be and how to get the type of man you want in our "Playbook Series" on www.glennsandifer.com. Book a session!

Ultimately, a man's goal should be to become a High-Value Man (a man of value or a productive man). Most readers will concentrate on the phrase *High-Value Man* and set that as the gold standard. It can be, but only roughly 5-10 percent of all men will be able to achieve this status. Most men should be comfortable with being a Man, and that can be a White-Collar, Blue-Collar, or Traditional Man.

Disclaimer: Not all men will achieve the status and title of High-Value Man. As stated, in most cultures, High-Value Men are between 5-10 percent of the total male population. However, if you are a woman reading this, your ultimate goal should be to find the right man for you. It may be in finding a High-Value Man, but it could also be with the other defined men. Note that, to find a High-Value Man, you must be a High-Value Woman. Men, bear in mind that to progress through each of these stages and achieve the desired outcome you seek, you must put in the work, so pay attention as we go along.

Boys Will Be Boys

We will discuss this in the next chapter, but remember middle school? Sure, you do. As a boy, you were busy playing outside, video games, sports, and hanging out with your friends. You went to school, and it was a great social outlet. You then began, for most, liking girls around sixth grade. When you did, you realized you were outmatched—outmatched intellectually, physically, and emotionally. This is the season in which boys develop their mindset around girls.

Boys are young at heart. They are still focused on the fantasies of their adolescence and/or teenage years. Boys spend most of their free time on boyish things, such as video games, sporting events, hanging with the guys, chasing dreams, and girls. For many, they are simply living in a state of delayed adolescence. A Boy will never satisfy a woman or a High-Value Woman. He will not be marriage-minded because he is a Boy. He will never be focused on the future because, in his mind, the future is now. He can only focus on those things before him without considering how to achieve more. He may be "stuck" in the moment, and while a female may want him to settle down or get serious, he can only think about satisfying his own needs at present. Singer Jorja Smith talks about dating this type of "Boy" in her song, "Teenage Fantasy." Her father warns her and asks her to look into her future to see where this "Boy" will be in years to come. Unless these boys transition into the next phases of their lives and move into manhood, their boyish desires and dreams will leave them stuck, living out their teenage fantasies.

We often hear Boys talking about their toys, cars, or trucks at family gatherings. They talk about where they will hang out this weekend or their next meal. Can you think of someone in your family or friend group who may be trapped in boyhood thoughts and actions? Have you seen them have a tantrum when what they want at the moment doesn't come to fruition? Maybe they are so wrapped up in their fantasy football league it's as if "they" are the ones on the field. Maybe this is you. Are you so consumed with the prospect of moving out of your mom's house one day, yet you have not developed a plan for how to do that? Sure, you may have a job and are making decent money, but have you thought about what steps will be required to make it on your own?

While it may be appropriate to think that a male in his twenties or even thirties has matured and should be ready to take on adulthood and, therefore, relationships, many fall into the category of Boy well into their adult years. If this is you and you are ready to progress to the next stage, keep reading. We will talk about several things you can do. The simple fact that you recognize these traits in yourself is a step in the right direction.

I Need A Hot Boy

Hot Boys, City Boys, and FCUK Boys and Boys have similar pursuits. The difference between a Boy and this version of a Boy is that they actually have the means to afford their fantasies. They spend just enough time working for money and working to win the attention of girls and women but never enough time to "earn" their complete attention. They have many excuses to justify why things haven't worked out. Their dreams are always one meeting or call away from coming to fruition. But that call never comes. They cannot make plans with a woman to save their lives, but they will try, and it will be half-assed.

For the most part, F Boys have graduated from most of their adolescent desires. However, now they have more discretionary income because they're typically in a job that allows them flexibility and freedom to act on the things they couldn't act on as a boy. An F Boy is the majority of the males that women find themselves attracted to because the F Boys are flashier. They're usually more hands-on. They're typically physically fit because many of them spend a lot of time in the gym or playing basketball. They're into yoga, Pilates, biking, or even overly obsessed with CrossFit. They have to be because their fitness keeps their options open with the opposite sex. Also, while they may still sound like a Boy, the big reason they're so into physical fitness is their end goal is purely one thing: to sleep with more women than their brother or best friend. And what attracts some women to them? Body. If you've been out at a bar, restaurant, or club, you certainly have seen them. F Boys are the loudest, the flashiest, the most active. They're the ones buying the drinks, bottles, and demanding VIP treatment. They are usually congregating in large packs of other F Boys, approaching women with a higher level of voracity. And they're all there for one thing: to get laid.

We see it all the time. Sarah chases an F Boy all through college because he is fun. He has some money, may be great in bed, and all her friends consider him "hot." She breaks up with him after college when she starts thinking about future plans because, although he is exciting and passionate, she realizes he will never be a true man. As she looks to her professional career, possibly settling down, the F Boy hasn't yet grown accustomed to just one woman but is still excited by the prospect of attracting many. All too often, however, the Sarahs of the world look up at 28 and realize they wasted many good years and a lot of energy on an F Boy who may be stuck in this stage of life for several more years.

He's Just Some Guy I Know

If he is not an F Boy, he may be in another category, **Guys or Dudes. This is a tricky stage, ladies, and the fellas will back me up. A guy** is typically very nice yet can be invisible to most women. Women, think about it. Do you know any Guys? Certainly, you do. You work with them, work out with them, see them around town at the store or car wash. You know them as "the nice guy that you run into at the coffee shop." But would you consider that nice guy to be dating material? Probably not. To most women, these men fall into the category of just a guy, having nothing special or noteworthy about him. He probably was a Boy or an F Boy at some point but grew out of that stage as he matured and started to desire something else in his life and in a woman, realizing women want more than just a good lay. As a method, he began putting away the childish pursuits of a boy and the selfish ways of an F Boy. He has actually taken the time to heal himself and look for forgiveness in those he's wronged. But, unlike F Boys, you don't want to "bake a cake with" a *Guy*.

We often hear women say, "I met this guy, and he is really nice, but there is just something missing." And the word that is often used is chemistry. "I don't feel like I have a lot of chemistry with him. He's a good friend. He's a really nice guy. He really listens. I feel like he's emotionally available, but there's no passion." He may only play basketball once a month and work out for health and fitness. Guys are not spending a bunch of money on unnecessary clothes or shoes or video games, so they are not flashy and, therefore, may not attract women's attention. Well, certain women anyway. From a competition standpoint and the sexual marketplace, Guys and Dudes don't get the best girls, but they're getting what would be deemed as lower-hanging fruit. They attract single mothers who are older or older women who have spent their twenties and early

thirties with the Boys and F Boys. While they are more stable than this latter group of males, they don't necessarily have the dreams and aspirations to make more of themselves. They are satisfied with the relationships these women can offer.

They Male It In

Now, where we find so many of today's modern men is the next category: Males. In 2020, around the world, the average rate of single parenthood is **seven percent**, which is under a third of the rate in the U.S. Over 80 percent of American kids in single-parent households live with their mother only, and that trend is growing. With males, you find that they have come from this environment at a higher rate than any other group.

You find a lot of former F Boys in this category because they have outgrown childish games but not emotional pursuits. Many men who were raised by single women find themselves in this category for decades of their lives. Males are much better communicators than Boys, F Boys, or Guys. They are often in touch with their feelings and often speak about how things make them feel. Not necessarily a Man of Action but not a pushover. You will find the bulk of these men know how to cook, clean, and keep a job and a home. They also are deferential to their women, having been influenced by more women than men in their lives. They are more than F boys and even more stable than guys or dudes. Unfortunately, many males are not stable enough to be fully respected by women at higher levels. This is a problem because many men have to overcome their "male" mentality.

Male Mentality, Not Mamba

Many males find they are not getting the relationship outcomes they want, and understanding this, they try to transition to a man. They

know how to acquiesce to strong women because their mother had to be strong. Their aunts and grandmother had to be strong. Life has taught them how to defer to women. He is accommodating, which is attractive because the F Boy was unavailable, the Boy was immature, and the Dude wasn't exciting. As a male, he may have F boy tendencies, but he's passed all the toxicity that typically comes out of the outward behavior. He's not on dating apps. He doesn't have a bunch of women running around. He doesn't have a bunch of children running around. He's working a really good job. He's pretty stable for the most part and might even be considered boring to some. He has a great relationship with his mother and his family. If a male grew up in a two-parent household, their dad was like this, keeping the peace, never challenging.

Males tend to be great communicators because they over-communicate. They are more in tune with their emotions, having been taught that emotions for a man are good because that's what the women that raised them wanted out of their men. Often their mothers dated and had children with F boys or Dudes and are now teaching their sons what they want in a relationship. Carrie, the mother in this example, would say to her son, "This is how a woman expects to be treated by a man," not knowing the tendencies discussed are far from traditional masculine outcomes. When a male goes to the dating market, he can get a girl but struggles to keep her because he's overly emotional, overly communicative, overly accommodating. Carrie, while raising her son to be this way, will not tolerate a non-traditional man in her own dating life! She is baffled as to why her son doesn't have better dating outcomes. It's because of you, Carrie.

Calling All The Real Men

When a Boy grows up or a Male gets it together, he is then considered a Man. In many instances, Men or former Males, are

Typically well-versed in and moving toward their purpose. They are obsessed with the outcome and will spend their free time on the outcomes they want. Men sometimes feel disconnected from the grind of a relationship because they are focused on their purpose. When a Man is working hard to succeed, it is better for both Men and Women. Men focus on manhood, family, legacy, and most will not rest until their goals are achieved. These men make the best husbands and fathers. These men struggle with Modern Women and High-Earning Women only because those groups tend to want a partnership. More on that later.

Looking at Men from the spiritual side, we know God created man. He had man and woman on His mind from the beginning, not as an afterthought as some may think. God created a woman to be a suitable helper after He saw Adam working. He was busy naming all the animals and all the items in the garden, and he had dominion over it. That is the type of man women look for. A man in the true, biblical sense of the word understands that, like Adam, who was in his calling, he too must be walking in his purpose to attract a woman who is a fit for him.

He must be productive for society. He is not just working a job but producing in it. He is making opportunities for others, pulling other people up. A Man is financially responsible and disciplined. In simple terms, he has discipline in his eating, health habits, and penis. Those habits of being with multiple women simultaneously were kicked to the wayside as he transitioned from a Male to a Man. A Man is attractive because he understands the importance and responsibility of caring for his woman and family. He is respected by other men, who recognize him as a peer. There is often a misconception among women that men strive to be successful for validation by women, but in reality, they are looking for validation from other like-minded men.

Men need to be productive to attract the right woman. You need to be in your purpose, and if you say you don't know what you want to do, you are not ready to walk in your purpose or take that leap to the next level. You can live a good life as a Male or Guy in a relationship that is less than your stated outcome or differential to the woman that chooses you. IF you want to be looked at as a peer among other men, you have to do the work to get there.

Most of us began dating at 15/16. When I started dating, I was a Boy. Even in college, I would consider myself as having been a Guy, at best, or a Male. As an adult, when I chose my first wife, I was a Male looking to be respected as a Man. This is an unrealistic expectation to purport to the population. Once I began doing the necessary work, I began to see the fruits of my investment. It takes work. This work is spiritual, financial, physical, emotional, and personal. It is your job to get the life you want, not anyone else's. I believe our greatest societal struggle is that personal accountability is lacking, and we often recognize it too late. In my case, neither my first wife nor I was ready to be in a relationship, let alone be married. Yet, there we were, trying to make a relationship work when the marriage was doomed to failure based on the stages we were in. This is where self-awareness and having other like-minded men around you help. After it was all said and done and I had filed for divorce, I looked back and realized I had married who I wanted at 16. What good is a 16-year-old's opinion when you are looking to get to 65?

I surrounded myself with like-minded, highly successful Men, knowing their influence would help me stay on the right path. If I wanted to find a Woman who had compatible characteristics with where I was going, I had to work to qualify for such a Woman.

"Qualify? What do you mean by qualify?" you might be asking. Yes, what type of woman do you qualify for? In other words, if you are an F Boy, do you think you have what it takes to be in a committed relationship with a High-Value Woman? If you are a Guy, do you qualify for a Woman? Since this might not make sense until we define a High-Value Woman, let's move on to the last category for males and see if you measure up to what is defined as a High-Value Man. Then you decide.

Who Are You Fighting For?

Only the top 10 percent *of all men* can be classified as High Value, putting them in the top tier of the dating hierarchy. These men have the luxury to wait and see what the market provides and then choose. They do this because they have chosen their purpose over everything. They live a life where they do not apologize for this decision and set a healthy boundary with their friends and family to support this. With the most important decision, choosing a significant other, this decision will either support or derail their progress.

Once you achieve the status of High-Value, it is important to maintain that status. These men will do whatever it takes to keep their status and thus legacies intact. This concept of a High-Value Man is not a new theory. It's been around since the '80s and is exclusive to men with specific characteristics:

1. A High-Value Man must earn at least a net of $12,500 a month for the previous four to five years. Money is not the only component, but it plays a major role in a High-Value Man walking in his purpose.
2. A High-Value Man surrounds himself with a group of like-minded men who share his ideals.

3. These men don't have to be married, but they should be in monogamous, committed relationships.
4. They are at the top of their game and their professions.
5. They continue to give back to others.
6. When married, High-Value Men are priests and prophets in their homes. They have a passion for their community and for giving back, knowing the importance of giving back with time and resources. The responsibility of a High-Value Man weighs heavily on his shoulders and, therefore, causes many men to cower from achieving this status.
7. He must be laser-focused on his purpose, which then aligns with his family's needs down the line. His wife and children must trust that he operates in his purpose and has their best interest at heart.

Although the number of men who aspire to become High-Value or those who believe they have achieved this level may be astounding, in reality, the degree of pressure and responsibility keeps this an exclusive group of less than 10 percent of the male population.

A High-Value Man has had to go through the proving round. This is where the characteristics above are developed. You may be a Blue-Collar Man. You can become a Blue-Collar High-Value Man. What it takes to make that leap is time. Unfortunately, few of us take the time to get to the level I am discussing. A White-Collar Man has to spend 7-10 years learning the politics, systems, and players of a multi-layered organization. A lawyer spends 10-15 years perfecting the arts of research, cross-examination, and closing arguments. What do these three have in common? It takes time.

While he is making these time investments, the High-Value Man has to position himself for not just the next opportunity but future ones. This could be through an engineering program, residency, or case. He also has to navigate his community and develop spiritually. With all this, he has to make sure his reputation remains impeccable. He has learned how to find his niche within the community, get involved, and be connected to the right people. He

Has consistently and diligently put in the work, building his reputation, increasing his earnings, becoming a leader, and mentoring others following in his footsteps, ultimately ascending to a High-Value status. The environment in which a High-Value Man maneuvers can be cutthroat, challenging, and difficult and therefore, excludes many men who strive to qualify for this category because of the difficulty. Not everyone is prepared to do what it takes to achieve this level of responsibility, and many fail or give up along the way, becoming content with their current situation. The High-Value Man has to find his niche and know when to call his shot. And with all of this – do you think this man should settle for just any spouse?

A High-Value Man is not exercising his options. In other words, discipline and fidelity in his relationship are important to him. His marriage is a covenant, a bond that cannot be broken. Some high-earning men, like politicians, entertainers, and athletes, cannot be classified as High-Value Men, not because of availability of resources, but due to their unwillingness to remain faithful and restrain from exercising their options. These men will attract only a certain kind of female, typically Girls or City Girls looking to be taken care of with the house, the cars, and amenities. Yet, they must be willing to accept that their man is emotionally unavailable or, as Beyonce says, won't "Put a Ring on It."

There are many places around the world where families struggle to give their children a chance at life. Here in the United States, we begin with a head start from a large percentage of our planet. Although we have more advantages and opportunities, simply because of our birth location, many people subscribe to a life of excuses and "blame splaining." This is a victim mentality that places the root cause of every problem anywhere but with themselves. People love to blame their parents, boss, and the government for their current lot in life. Taking trauma off the table,

The position you find yourself in today is not necessarily someone else's fault. In fact, it is completely within your control to change your circumstances. The beauty of therapy is you can learn to cope with your past mistakes and failures, overcome self-limiting beliefs, identify shortcomings, and develop a plan to move beyond where you are to where you want to go. Although I am not a therapist or medical professional, I am a strong advocate for everyone seeking therapy to help them identify negative perceptions, overcome obstacles, and step into their purpose.

Here we have choices, options, and solutions available to each of us. We must exercise our right to make decisions as to how we want to live our lives. Do you want to remain stuck or unhappy? What type of man do you aspire to be? The type of woman you attract and marry, if that is your desire, or maintain a committed relationship with depends on you and your decisions and choices. Do you want a woman who supports you in your endeavors and stands by your pursuits? Or are you only interested in a one-night stand, satisfying an immediate need without regard for the future?

Today, as a High-Value Man, the relationships I seek out must be mutually reciprocal. I finally got to the point where I was comfortable putting some toxic relationships where they needed to be, knowing I wanted more for my life and my relationship. How do the men in your life impact who you will become? Do they bring you up or drag you down? Carefully consider your friend group as you identify what type of man you aspire to be and how that will impact the type and quality of woman for whom you will qualify.

Key Takeaway

If you are a woman reading this chapter, consider the type of relationship outcomes you have experienced and the type of man to whom you are attracted. Maybe that is the type of man you qualify

For now. In the next chapter, we will take a closer look at the stages of womanhood, how to identify the man you qualify for, and how to vet men to achieve the outcome you desire. It may be that Mr. Right is out there, and you are the problem that has been holding you back from finding him.

Chapter 3

Girls To High-Value Women

You are a woman or want a woman. As in the previous chapter, that is my best guess because you are still here! To move forward, I need to recalibrate your understanding of the word *woman.*

There is a difference in the female species with various types of women, each wondering why they can't find a mate. Men and women don't realize they fall into these categories that then may hold them back from finding true love. Upbringing, expectations, financial status, and desires impact the relationship outcomes they achieve. In the following pages, we will talk about each of the six types of women, their characteristics, and therefore, the expectations of each.

Women, know that no matter which category you find yourself in, you can make a change and achieve the relationship outcome you desire if, in fact, you *want* to make a change in your life. I will tell you how, so keep reading. These categories of women, of course, correspond to various categories in which men fall as well, as

Outlined in the previous chapter, the misalignment of which causes a breakdown in communication and disconnect in relationships.

Just as with males, there are six types of women in the dating environment: Girls, Hot Girls or City Girls, Gals or Chicks, Females, Women, and High-Value Women. Unfortunately, men have never been taught to differentiate between the types of women. Men often find themselves confused, chasing the wrong type of woman, and unsatisfied in their relationships. I raise the question again to the men out there: What type of woman do you qualify for? I raise the question to the women reading: What type of Woman are you?

Let's take a look at the common characteristics of the female species, figure out where you fit and what type of man you qualify for. Have you been looking for that pot of gold at the end of the rainbow? Like the male species, women have to take a good, hard look at themselves before they wish or hope for the "man of their dreams."

Baby Girl – She Ain't Ready

Do you remember middle school? This is around the time when boys and girls really started to like each other. For me, it was in sixth grade. We had classes on both the main floor and the second floor in the back of the school. This meant your locker could be on either floor. And each locker hallway had its own culture. Depending on your taste, you would know when to navigate those halls. This is important because this is when girls would all decide which boy was the "IT" boy that week. Translation, girls all like the same boy. They would talk about the same boy during first period, study hall, gym, lunch, and on the bus ride home. Now, I was not a boy the girls ever liked (surprising, I know), and it was certainly overwhelming from the boys' perspective, waiting your turn, not knowing what to expect. Girls were the drivers of all the culture, talks, and activities

During this time. Also, it was overwhelming when they no longer liked you! How upset were the poor guys that found out they were no longer the "IT" guy and that the girls had moved on to someone new? These are Baby Girls, and they are driven by three things: Feelings, Fantasies, and Friends.

Feelings Over Facts

At that age, the emotions of a Baby Girl will drive your entire life as a boy. She typically first communicates her feelings like this: "I don't want to…" – "I don't like to…" – "I don't want to go…" A Girl has a vision based on her feelings. This vision is based on what boys are supposed to be like or how boys are supposed to treat them. As such, they quickly moved on once they realized that we boys did not live up to their imagined expectations. Even at that young age, "relationships" for us boys were challenging. Boys have no emotional intelligence to show them how to navigate feelings. Now, if you have great emotional maturity, you are not a Girl. But even if you do, please understand your feelings are your responsibility, not that of your mother, father, sister, or boy!

What's Your Fantasy?

In the illustrious words of Chris Bridges, aka Ludacris, "What's Your Fantasy?" If you are familiar with the song, you see that the boy is asking the girl what her fantasy is. As a matter of fact, like most boys today, he is telling the girl what her fantasy *should* be – and describing it in great detail. **Girls** are young at heart, still focusing their free time on the fantasies of adolescence. They may dream about the wedding, house, car, clothes, makeup, but they are not yet marriage-minded. They are interested in the outcomes related to relationships, marriage, and family, since they were taught early. Girls know the

Result of all the effort with the boy should be house, kids, husband, and not necessarily in that order. A Girl can easily be disillusioned when her reality does not match her fantasy as life happens. You know these Girls. You may be this Girl or have raised this Girl. The challenge for this Girl is to move past fantasy and into reality. But that is not the real drive; it is what comes next.

Your feelings keep you unfocused on your future! Now, remember, girls develop much faster emotionally and intellectually than boys. You don't need a study with facts, data, or statistics to know that; you can look over your own life for that information. But a Girl is rarely focused on her future due to a false sense of security that she has time. You don't. Girls Don't. Guys, girls don't have as much time as they believe. The biological clock is ticking. Geriatric Pregnancy is diagnosed at age 35. If you spend your twenties and early thirties playing in Feelings and Fantasies, you run the risk of missing your window. Speaking from a space of aspiration is fine, but without concrete plans to achieve your result, you are just that: Talking! No one, not even the next group, Hot Girls, wants to deal with that.

This group also, because of their Fantasies, believes "Prince Charming" is right around the corner. He is not. The reality is that the Girl has not considered what she brings to the table or any quality about this man that would be attractive to her. Although both Boys and Girls are focused on fantasies and youthful endeavors, Girls have to realize the outcome and benefits of relationship and marriage are attainable but not without doing the work. And no one holds you back from doing the work like this next group: Friends.

Friends, How Many of Us Have Them?

Remember, Girls know the result of dating should be commitment, which leads to marriage, kids, and a husband. What happens when one Girl begins to move in that direction, and her friends do not? Well, it's not what you think; they tend to "rationalize" that they want their friend to be successful, too! Now, the ironic part of this entire thought process is that your "Friends" will leave you high and dry as soon as a "Boy" makes his interest known. And some "Good Girls" tend to neglect something early that can lead them to the outcome they desire. Girls can also place a boy last on their priority list when it comes to personal pursuits, especially when their friends have undue influence. This does not change the fact that Girls often still chase boys, but no boy is ever good enough – for their FRIENDS. How toxic is this? She is supposed to be your girl, but when she and a couple of friends get finished sizing up your boy, he is nothing! Don't let this happen to you; keep your friends in the friend zone and let your boy chase you!

Be focused on the future. Do not let your feelings, fantasies, or friends keep you single! Now, the next group will take a dramatic turn. As we discuss, don't get in your feelings. As my grandmother said, "Only a hit dog hollers."

She's A Hot Girl, Living For The City

"What you need, boy? I need a hot girl. What you want, boy? I want a hot girl." If you haven't noticed, we will take a lot from hip hop culture in this book. But what does this song teach us? Boys want Hot Girls. Before I get into this category, those of you triggered, please breathe. There is *nothing wrong with being a City Girl*. If you are a City Girl, be okay with your outcomes. Be okay with the life you have created and the life you sustain. A City Girl is not

Only the name of a popular hip hop group but the lifestyle of many. Think "HOT GIRL SUMMER," or "Warm Aunty Winter." Now, back to the book. What is a Hot Girl? As of this writing, the term is used for what's also known as a City Girl.'

Now, what do both of these girls have in common? According to the Hot Boys or Cash Money Millionaires, a Hot Girl is silent, violent, yet jazzy and classy. She will grab her Hot Boy and make sure she takes charge. She will go to jail if needed to protect what is hers. A City Girl is an adult female. Unlike the Girl, this female has the means to afford the fantasies of adolescence. Like the Hot Boy, F Boy (as already discussed), she is going to be sure her money is secure. Above, I used the words of HOT BOYZ to express what she has and how she moves. The difference between a Girl and a City Girl is they can afford those fantasies. In many other respects, Hot Girls or City Girls are similar to Dudes. She can pull the Range Rover off the lot quickly, yet still check a disrespectful chick. Now, what is this really saying, full of contradictions, chaos, and C.R.E.A.M.?

Wait, You Just Said…

Not you but your friend, why is she always stating one thing but doing another? She left her ex, but now you see a post on social media, professing her love. She always gets into it with her supervisor, yet is always staying late to help out? And this will sting; she wants to lose weight but is always at Whataburger. How? Why? A contradiction is a combination of statements, ideas, or features opposed to one another. She is that! Full of contradictions. Why? Because, as a City Girl, her life has been set up to be this way. Listen, women are the freest they have ever been at any time in history. Especially in the Western world, women have more money, influence, access, power, and conveniences that make choices seem infinite. But, with freedom comes responsibility. With freedom comes choice and tradeoff. When this City Girl chooses, she often

Chooses incorrectly, which leads to her being full of contradictions. But that's not the worst part; contradictions often lead to chaos.

Chaos Theory

The Chaos Theory in mathematics states that complex systems whose behavior is highly sensitive to slight changes in conditions, with small alterations can give rise to great consequences. These are the words of Oxford, not me! You know a cousin or friend that is always in a state of chaos? City Girls have similar pursuits to Girls. This lack of awareness, which is the sexiest thing any woman can wear, leads to bad outcomes. Those outcomes lead to chaos in their lives. They lose clients left and right. They are out of school; they switch entry- level jobs at the first sign of trouble. And here is the strangest part. They often see themselves as victims. Victims of their mother's bad choices, the school they went to, racism, sexism, patriarchy. It doesn't matter because the delusion around their fantasy of what their life should be leads them to dissatisfaction. If they do have children, this group creates the lion's share of the next two groups. Their children are the true victims and say things like, "Mom can't keep it together for us." She is "doing the best she can," but is she? If a life is chaotic, it is due to conditions that have slight changes that lead to consequences. And the consequences are the biggest problem. But their solution to the problem is not counseling or accountability. It is C.R.E.A.M.

Cash Rules Everything Around Me. You saw C.R.E.A.M, and your mind went left! Own it and move on. Coined by the Iconic Wu-

Tang Clan, cash rules everything around me; get the money, dollar, dollar bill y'all. The efforts all lead to having enough cash to support dreams, family, and self. They have the car, the apartment or condo, the makeup, hair, and clothes of which they have always dreamed. They spend just enough time working a job to afford these things, making their aspirations a reality, yet they don't have many

Responsibilities. They have an image of what they want in life, the lifestyle they want to live, the Man, Man of Value, or High-Value Man they want to meet, but they have not done the work within themselves to qualify for this type of man.

With the City Girl or Hot Girl, this is the truth. You will always see and hear of the next dream or hustle. This is not opinion because, even though life is full of contradictions or chaotic, they will *never* fumble their bag. Girls in this group, since they are full of contradictions, are often "Entrepreneurs" because they are always building a client list or business. Now, the endeavor is rarely, if ever, Microsoft Lite. It is usually real estate, insurance, janitorial services, vending machines, or online retail. Separately, these are great pursuits in addition to consistent income, especially if passive, but remember, this group is full of contradictions and chaos. They can never get it to the point of passive. It always takes their time and energy investment. How did they get this way, where contradictions, chaos, and C.R.E.A.M rule their lives?

The Hot Girl or City Girl mindset often begins in middle and high school. Remember the story from the Girls section? These same girls spend adolescence discussing clothing, jewelry, and makeup. These girls are the ones that partied with the older guy from high school or the guy that didn't finish his junior year. Even her first boyfriend may be an older boy who dotes on her, providing her with the kind of lifestyle she aspires to have. He becomes the archetype of what she believes love is, so she over-invests in the boy. Unfortunately, if it fails, this boy becomes the stereotypical toxic relationship, hardening her to future opportunities. Unfortunately for other men, this relationship has left a sour taste in her mouth. Although she wants to be respected for the struggles she has been through with men, she secretly considers men as replaceable and/or trash. And who can blame her? She spent those early years investing in the wrong guy. She hasn't invested the time in herself

To qualify for any level of a man higher than a Boy or F Boy, who consequently is not giving her the attention she craves, and High- Value Men don't have time to accommodate her needs. This ground does best with a fellow City Boy or at best a Guy. Those two groups accommodate this foolishness. Otherwise, you will find many women in the next group.

Gal Pal

Do you all remember My Buddy and Kid Sister? If you are not an eighties baby, probably not, but please check out the link on www.glennsandifer.com/videos/kidsister/mybuddy "Kid Sister/Kid Sister/Kid Sister/ Wherever I go, she goes/Kid Sister/Kid Sister/Kid Sister/ Kid Sister and Me." This was a great song and, from what I remember, a very popular toy. My cousins all had a Kid Sister, and it was *the* toy during elementary show and tell. It was always popular with the Girls and was always there growing up. That's what a Gal Pal is like in adulthood.

Not unlike City Girls, **Gals or Chicks** are very nice. Most men know a lot of them. They work with Chicks, work out with Chicks, hang out with Chicks, and sleep with Chicks. Men seek them out and believe they would be a nice wife or girlfriend. But she can't be. She is a Chick. She is just a gal you know, met, or went out on a date with. And just like Kid Sister, everywhere you go, she goes. If you show up at the gym, she is there, available, and ready to help you with your chest press and cardio. There is nothing really alarming or special about this group. Men, Men of Value, and High-Value Men know a lot of Gals but don't really see them as a girlfriend or a wife

Long-term. They are kind of boring, homely even. Something is missing, maybe that spark or chemistry. They don't have the look or the attraction a Man or High-Value Man wants. Let's look at an example with our good friend Tim.

Don't Do It Tim!

Tim has an idea of what he wants. He is attracted to a woman at the gala or charity function. However, the Chick he met at the coffee shop does not fit that. It does not have to be that she is dull or wears very little makeup. Maybe she has let herself go a little or even has more guy friends than girls. Many Gals or Chicks are labeled as funny or fun to hang out with. She may play Madden or is a sneakerhead.

But at the end of the day, no one wants someone who's just funny or another pal. Men don't look at the Gal or Chick as something to be desired.

Lastly, she is overly horny and makes it known. She makes herself available, even expressing a sense of desperation that was not apparent in the Hot Girl or Girl. They have not successfully obtained the relationship outcomes they want and are self-aware of their shortcomings. More importantly, they are ok with them. They may accept that they make a modest $40,000 a year, are a little overweight, but have a nice personality. These women find and marry guys and ultimately have long-lasting, basic relationships. They have no phenomenal outcomes, no phenomenal kids. But they're together and happy, and there is nothing wrong with that if that is where you are the most content.

Once a Gal or Chick puts in the work to achieve the relationship outcome she has wanted, she will easily settle into the role of a wife because she knows the work that she did to get in. The cautionary tale in this scenario is that they stop working once they get the relationship outcome. However, it is fair to say the Gal or Chick has the best potential of landing someone out of all the groups, a Guy or sometimes a Man. But beware, some Gals allow bitterness and hurt to lead them to the next category.

Femme Fatale –

I like the Oxford Dictionary. It ensures we begin the discussion from a place of good faith. Defined by Oxford, a Femme Fatale is an attractive and seductive woman, especially one who is likely to cause distress or disaster to a man who becomes involved with her. Enter the Female. Many single women have raised this next group called **Females.** Sure, by nature, you are a female, but there is something special about being a Female versus just another member of the female species. Many strong single mothers have raised this group. They are excellent at communicating but are usually very emotional. They are led by their emotions and expect understanding around these emotions. They are typically more stable professionally and financially because their parents taught them to be independent, not interdependent. Females are not women who depend on a man, cooperate with a man, or are deferential to a man. They often meet men who are in shock and awe about how much they have accomplished, yet they struggle to attract and retain the Man, Man of Value, or High-Value Man. But

Why? Well, it could be because of number, numbness, and negativity.

Too Many In Here

This is by far the largest group with whom I have spoken. Many will tell you when hearing these characteristics, they cringe. They might say, "What does my mother have to do with my outcome? If the men I met would only commit and remain consistent, then I wouldn't have these outcomes." Remember, there are too many because, unfortunately, in most communities in the West, we have single-parent households. This is of no fault of the child but is the fault of their parents. Two adults should be able to figure it out, but most times, when kids are involved, they can't figure it out. Thus, this is the largest number of any group of women. This leads to confidence that the issue can't be within themselves; it has to be with the men they encounter. Wrong! The men they have encountered often run due to their emotional outbursts and inconsistencies. And besides, with the sheer number of available women, those men believe the grass is always greener. If not, what about numbness?

I Have Become Numb To All This

Having poor relationship outcomes can lead to many things. But for this group, the main outcome is numbness. You know this female. She is often unimpressed or unbothered by many things. But in reality, she is totally pressed and bothered by it all. To cope, she develops the lifestyle trait of numbness. This is unhealthy because you miss out on good Men, who can provide the relationship outcome you seek. They think, "Work is okay, family is okay, money is okay, health and fitness are okay. Why even bother? I don't want to put in the effort because my outcomes never arrive.

This is so unfair!" Plus, this group sees their friends level up and have the outcomes they seek. Oh, they are always in a wedding party each Spring and Summer. They are happy for their friend as a new bride but silently and with the other Females complain about why it won't work for them. And if not numb, they express their dissatisfaction with negativity...

A Negative Nancy (Karen)

Now we all know what a Karen is. Karens are irrespective of race, socio-economic status, creed, religion, or age. Karens are all over social media, disrupting happy experiences because of their own bias. We had Cookout Karen, Water Cooler Karen, Child Care Karen, and Wrong Number Karen just to name a few, but the Negative Karen or Negative Nancy takes the cake. *Nothing* satisfies this female. Remember, girls are more advanced with the development of emotions. And as Girls mature or move past City Gir or Gal behavior, their emotions grow with their experiences. As a Female, most, unfortunately, don't yet understand the power of their emotions. Emotions should be managed with dignity and without destroying those around them. There is grace in learning the importance of managing their emotions with dignity to get the outcomes they want. While Females are hyper-focused on their emotions, they're not prepared to deal with those emotions. Yet, they expect the man they are with to manage all their emotions. That man's job becomes about managing her emotions rather than simply loving her. This is the group of women that typically say, "I'm a strong, independent woman, and I don't need a man."

The reason they say that is men have let them down. Their father let them down; their uncles let them down; their brother let them down. When they were a Girl, their first boyfriend let them down. When they were a City Girl, The F Boy let them down. Their mom let them down. Anyone in authority has let them down, and the women

In their lives have taught them that men are interchangeable. They have a utility, and their utility is money and sex, not caring about what the man thinks or desires.

All Together Now

As of this writing, women span a total of five Generations: Traditionalist, Baby Boomers, Gen X, Millennials, and Gen Z. Many believe they don't need a man because they are fully capable of surviving on their own. The world is so safe now with so many conveniences that have led to the correct conclusion that they can make it on their own. These women have experienced some satisfaction with independence. We often see females wake up at 40, look at their life and their relationship outcomes and ask, why don't I have a mate? They're attractive. They work out. Females do very well professionally because it doesn't require them to deal with their emotions. They've done everything the female needed to do to attract a man. Like the City Girl, they know how to make money. Although they have mastered being an adult, Females have not yet mastered their emotions and the necessary emotional output to maintain a relationship. But be careful!

When they do get married, they typically marry a Guy or an F Boy, a Guy because he is available, an F Boy because he is flamboyant, dramatic, and charismatic. An F Boy knows what to say to get this woman to respond, and since they're not invested in emotions, they don't care if she has emotional outbursts. In fact, an F Boy is not equipped to deal with her emotions. This group benefits the most from therapy and learning to deal with their emotions and past trauma to take them to the next level.

We also see many women in this category never marrying or marrying and divorcing multiple times. By not dealing with trauma or emotions, they cannot genuinely connect with a man to achieve

The outcome they are looking for. Sure, Females appear to have it all together; they are financially secure, have a great career, and take care of themselves and their bodies. While the fact that she is chronically single may be astounding to some based on outward appearances alone, it is her internal *you* and unresolved issues and emotions preventing her from being truly happy. Now, this group does have the highest propensity to move past this stage and become their true nature, Woman.

I AM WOMAN

"I am Woman" was released in 1971 by Helen Reddy. The song became an anthem of the Feminist Movement. She even performed it on *Soul Train*! Why? You know why. "I am woman, hear me roar/In numbers too big to ignore/and I know too much to go back and pretend/cause I've heard it all before." Oh my God! What does this thinking do to relationships? I believe many great things came from and continue to come from

the Feminist Movement. Ruth Bader Ginsburg, Title IX, the WNBA, and more women in the workplace. None of this should impact how we relate to one another, but you and I both know that to be false. Women come in three types: Traditional, Modern or High-Value.

Traditional Women – Who Can Find?

The Bible says to be fruitful and multiply. To get to the status of a Man, Man of Value or High-Value Man, the male must be fruitful and multiply everything he has. To be fruitful and multiply requires partnership with people and ultimately requires a partnership with their significant other. A man needs to find a woman, and a woman needs to find a man.

A Girl will transition to a Traditional Woman if she has been trained properly by a mother, an auntie, or grandmother to understand the impact of positive womanhood! For a Traditional Women, serving her husband and family is her main purpose. The Bible says a woman is a suitable helper – not a suitable administrator, not suitable CEO, not a suitable vice-president of diversity and inclusion – a suitable helper. When it comes to your relationships, the key word should be about helping.

The Helper Model – A Trad Woman's Dream

What is the Helper Model? To all my Christian women, let's talk for real. You were created with a mandate; Adam and Eve, male and female, were on the mind of God as He was creating us. Adam was done being fruitful and multiplying, and a deep sleep fell on him. And

God said it's not good for man to be alone. What type of man? A man like Adam, who was in a relationship with God, was productive, fruitful, and multiplying. He was doing God's will and working in the area where God had called him, the garden of Eden. God gave Eve to Adam for companionship and help.

Let's look at it this way, women. If you are in a relationship with a man and really want it to work, stop and ask, am I his companion? Am I helping? However, we know the word 'help' can be triggering too, and many women will say, "I don't want to help him." "Why should I help him?" "He needs to be a full man on his own in order to keep me." Now it's not really about the help but rather the question, do you value men? If your answer is No, then my advice is to stay out of the dating market and stop pretending you want to be married. You are not qualified for a traditional man if you are not of the mindset to be his helper.

Why This Matters

Let's look at an example of how a man wants help. Let's say he's an attorney on the partner track. His help is going to come from you being at home, available and understanding that, at six o'clock on a Thursday, the senior partner is going to call him in and want him to come out to have drinks with a client. While his success is dependent upon his commitment, you benefit from the partner track as his wife. This would be the same scenario for a 28-year-old doctor. He has finished his residency, been placed in a hospital, taken care of himself physically, and has begun to make a dent in his student loan. He now believes he is ready to begin dating to find a wife. The woman will first have to understand that he's on call while he is on track to be a high earner in his profession. Adaptability and flexibility are the help he needs.

You will not often find a marriage that works when both parties are high-level executives, attorneys, or doctors, which leads to competition, fighting, and misunderstanding. The man needs the woman at home, managing the home, the kids, on the same page as he is, placing her professional pursuits in the back seat until he achieves his career success. The woman is, in this case, the much-needed help to allow the man to be fruitful and multiply.

The purpose of this book is to help a woman and a man identify who they are, what they're dealing with, and what they qualify for. To do that, you need The Modern Ground to come to the proverbial table with something and understand what that person is thinking and vice versa. If you don't come with that piece, you're not trying to come. You're not operating in good faith, and you're not trying to reach The Modern Ground. Therefore, Women are well-versed and moving towards their aspirations, education, and career.

Modern Women – Not As Bad As You've Been Told

Modern Women are former Girls or Females. Women are never made from City Girls! Women are well-versed in moving towards their aspirations. Education, career and relationship pursuits are prime directives. They are more obsessed with the outcome of all pursuits than the journey. Women have done the work to move past traumas and don't make that the responsibility of everyone else!

Women are often frustrated with their standing, position, or role and often challenge Males or Men in public settings. They will sometimes feel disconnected from relationships, whether a high earner or a moderate earner. Modern Women want "partnerships" or "50/50" relationships. When Modern Women discuss a relationship, it is in regard to tangible benefit: what's in it for me? Learning, growing or developing with an individuals is not the key outcome. It is their growth and their service! Accountability is like kryptonite to this group.

We often hear women say, "I got my own, and I don't need a man." "I take trips." This is not limited to city girl behavior, modern women often level this up.

So, this group is typically looking for a partner. As I mentioned earlier, a man's role is about service and protection. That is his duty. If a woman wants a partner, a 50/50 relationship, she needs to be about service too. Now, I get it; you may be hating on me right now, thinking, "I'm not serving anyone!" However, let's look at what service means in the traditional sense.

So, let's get back to this category of Women, who are typically looking for partners. A partner is someone who's going to split the responsibilities, including the house, kids, finances, and most importantly, the difficult task of emotional support. If the men are trying to lead, and they find someone who is looking for a partner, clearly, this relationship is not going to work. Partners need to be with partners. Leaders need to be with helpers, and helpers need to be with leaders. Men and High-Value Men don't want a partnership; they are looking for women who relish the opportunity to be helpers.

Women try to convince men of what they want and need when, in reality, there is a misalignment of qualifications based on expectations and outcomes. If a woman goes into a relationship with a High-Value Man, expecting him to be a partner in the home, available whenever she wants, and ready and willing to split responsibilities 50/50 with her, she is setting herself up for a poor and disappointing relationship outcome. In other words, she will spend her time upset, wondering why he is not more available, dependable, and invested in their relationship. On the other hand,

women don't like accountability, which also impacts their relationship outcomes. This is important with a Woman and not the other groups because a Woman is what a man and a High-Value Man needs.

Who's That Pokémon? Or What Do You

Do you all know what a Pokémon is? In the cartoon at a commercial break there was a title card that showed the outline of a Pokémon. Now fans of the show would know based on that outline which Pokémon was being presented. That presentation was exciting when you returned from commercial break as you wanted to determine if you were right? That is what is like for Modern Men cheking for modern women: WHO"S THAT POKEMON? Well, there are three versions of Modern Women: Boss Chick, Baddies and DIVAS. Get your popcorn ready!

Boss Chick

The main version of the Modern Women, Modern Men Meet! A Boss Chick is one that knows her worth based on her profession and will be sure a Modern Man knows it too! A Boss Chick has her money, career, and goals together. Remember, Women in general and Modern Women in particular have moved past the traumas that impact Females. This keeps them ahead in the dating game. Modern Women want 50/50 and Boss Chicks are no different! She knows how to hold her own and never lets anyone talk down to her. She expects respect from all, since he is an independent and self-sufficient. She knows the lifestyle she wants, achieves it, and aims for the finer things. Most Boss Chicks are "solopreneurs" of their own agency. This is not to be dismissed out of turn. It takes hard work and dedication to hunt in our society. But once you do, you find that hunting becomes easier. Other Women look at this group as their prototype. They make well over 150K adjusted for inflation in their local area. They can buy what they want when they want. They can take a trip when they want, making sure their clients/business/employees know it. They see themselves as a beacon of hope for all versions of women and should be highly regarded. The problem comes when the Boss Chick dates a Traditional or High-Value Man. The rest of the men discussed will never qualify for this woman. She Bad, She Bad, She Bad She Bad - Baddies

So now that we know what a Boss Chick is, let's define the next group. A Baddie is a female that works only to care for her unit. This can include herself, parent(s) and children. She is obsessed with appearance. The Modern Woman that goes for BBLS and has a $5,000 a month beauty fund is in this group. Her friends and family are her driving factor. Baddies differ from the Boss Chick because they are always employees, but are highly compensated for their effort. A Baddie does not have her own agency. She is usually attached to a Boss Chick or a High-Value Man, professionally. She will be submissive to either of these to ensure her money is not compromised. Baddies only want Reformed Bad Boys that are Modern Men. Since she is Modern, she expects 50/50 in dating. Make it make sense? Now, Guys and City Boys love this group of women. Why may you ask? It is because work is work and play is play. This group often conflates their experiences with Boys and F Boys with *all* Men. They are pretty, so why are they not getting the results they want? Your Hot Girl Summer comes heavily from this subgroup. It is never this group's fault when they have poor relationship outcomes. This is the largest group of the Modern Woman.

I'M A D..a..Diva. – Divas

We have Boss Chicks and Baddies, now we must turn our attention to the DIVAS. The popular song by Beyonce Knowles: Diva. This was an anthem in the 2000s. And just like that song, this group is the most annoying to all other Women: Modern, Traditional and High-Value. Diva is a female that is pretty, holds herself in high regard, and expects you to do the same. They have not earned that respect or regard, but demand it all the same. She is often confusing to the market: she seems like a City Girl, but has all the expectations of a Modern Women. She has many options for "entertainment" when it comes to Boys, F Boys, Guys, and Males. And why wouldn't she? She is everything they want her to be! Let that sink in. She has her money together, is usually involved in her community, has a great standing with her family and friends, and is looked at as the prototype. She does not need a man for anything but the utility she decides. And if she chooses a man, he better be appreciative. The thing that differentiates the DIVA from the Baddie is the need for utility. This is what is common with a City Girl.

This version of a Modern Women, often entertains Males and F Boys. She does linger a bit to long with a Male and often leaves him for a true Modern Man. The creative class of employee is usually considered a DIVA. This is where you find your hair dressers, estetichians, make up artist, dancers and singers. They are artistic and lead with their emotions. Making them seem unlike a Modern Woman, but also will dismiss anyone that dares to challenge them.

She will not discriminate professionally, but he also has to be aspiring for more. Her man can be a long-haul driver, work at the Amazon Warehouse, or some other Blue-Collar Profession, just as long has he is looking to own it one day. Again, as a 50/50 Partner she would love for that man to elevate on her watch. It feeds the ego that she upgraded him. If he makes $50K per year, she wants him to "level up" to $150K within a designated time period. This causes conflict in her relationships because Modern Men who are happy with their profession and earnings, won't move up to please her.

Precious And Valuable – High Value Women

This is the most sought after group of Women. The High-Value Woman is the top 10% of all women in any society! Now when we thing of this, like High-Value Men, the **High-Value Woman** makes has the ability to select any version of a male. At any given time, but she only selects a long-term relationship with a High-Value Man. Remember, here we believe that the best relationship outcome is a relationship between one (1) man and one (1) woman with marriage, children and legacy as the result. They choose the purpose of cooperating with and supporting a High-Value Man in *his* purpose. They are the pick of the litter and support the leaders at any organization, including the head of the household. High-Value Women run the lives behind the scenes of High-Value Men, yet lead with femininity, inspiration, beauty, and cooperation. Even though they have it, they never lead with education, career, influence, or money. While most women want to be considered High-Value Women, they are, in fact, a rare breed.

The theory is that, if a woman wants a relationship, she wants him to be high-value. She wants him to have influence, to be a provider and a protector. If she has religious beliefs, she wants him to be the priest or prophet at home while also professing his belief. We call this the Four Ps in Part 2.

Right there and say, "I don't care what the man wants. He needs to want me." That is the conflict many relationships face.

High-Value Women understand the most important need of their High-Value Man: cooperation. We are not talking about obedience. We are talking about being the helper, cooperative, and allowing him to lead. Respectful cooperation can go a long way! A High-Value Woman understands the difference between following her own pursuits and reaping the benefits of supporting her High-Value Man to achieve his. A High-Value Man's number one priority is his purpose, which will then afford him the ability to care for their relationship, their children, and their family legacy. In that order. Modern Women, Gals, Females, Girls, and City Girls don't like where they rank in the priority list and expect and want to be higher than they should be. Traditional Women are not interested in the purpose of a High-Value Man. Her understanding of her purpose defines a High-Value Woman in the order. We often see, as men mature to this level, their women are still expecting them to show up as a Guy, Male, or Man. It doesn't work, and these Men need their Women to step up to the plate.

High-Value Women are post the pursuits of adolescence, past emotional traumas and petty squabbles. A High-Value Man doesn't have time to be caught up in emotions, fantasies, or even a woman that's obsessed with her own outcomes. He wants a High-Value Woman, and nothing less, to be cooperative, supportive, and helpful as he walks in his purpose. Women, ask yourself, "Am I willing to forego my professional career to assist and support my husband in his purpose?" Notice the use of husband here. If not, know that he is a valuable commodity and can pursue any woman he wants. However, consider how you lead and then ask yourself what type of man you qualify for. Do you lead with femininity, inspiration, and beauty? A High-Value Man wants a High-Value Woman. He can sleep with a Chick or a City Girl. He won't even talk to a Girl because it's too frustrating.

When a High-Value Woman meets her mate, she is not engaged for two years. She is married in six months because she understands she's rare, and the man interested in her is rare. This is why you find a lot of arranged marriages in different cultures. This concept will become more in vogue in the U.S. in the foreseeable future because, as there is a higher percentage of older, single women, younger women look on and want to change. They want to be happy with their relationship outcomes, and by reading books like this, they understand how to do it.

SMV – Why High-Value Women Win

The SMV or sexual marketplace value is a term that has popped up over the past several years. It states there is an inverse relationship between peak attraction between men and women. Women reach their SMV Peak at a younger age. This is typically between 20-33. Men reach their SMV Peak at a much older age. This is typically between 35-50. What a difference! High-Value Women understand this equation, do not argue against it and operate under the principle.

This is why High-Value Women typically marry older. It has nothing to do with him, it has everything with her choosing HIM. Her value, her sexual marketplace value, tends to decline as she gets closer to 40. If you disagree with the Sexual Marketplace Value, you are not alone. There are countless videos, articles and reports on this. As a Modern Woman, you don't have to start an empire or become a mogul. Sadly, other groups of women look at that as slavery or indentured servitude. In reality, the High-Value Woman will step right into her place beside her husband, receiving acclaim, fortune, and respect as she stands beside him in his purpose and pursuits.

I GOT THESE DEGREES!

Although a High-Value Woman does not have to have many degrees, she has some education to know how to operate and move within her man's spaces. She knows how to cook and clean and is not stressed by a crying baby. She doesn't walk out of the house without polish on her fingernails or toes. She leans into her femininity but is not flashy or scantily clad. Most High-Value Women work and make good money, but their career does not

Define them. Their end goal is a thriving family with at least 2.5 kids and a respected man in the community.

My grandfathers were older than both of my grandmothers. They went to war, came back, bought houses, and had children. They put the kids through college, paid for cars, and retired comfortably. This was before looks, attraction, and chemistry became the calling card to success. Unfortunately, every group outside of the High-

Value Woman is focused on that. "I need to be attracted to them. You have to look a certain way. I have to feel a certain way around him. You have to make me feel this way." These are all superficial things that don't get to the root of the purpose of the relationship. Men cannot have the same expectation of a High- Value Woman or a Woman as they had with a Female or a City Girl.

Key Takeaway

Just as there are differences between types of men and what type of woman they qualify for, women, ask yourselves, what type of woman are you and what type of man do you qualify for? Am I willing to be a helper and support my man? While money is a major factor in determining men's positional relationships, a woman's value is determined by her willingness and ability to support his purpose. Ultimately, she will reap the benefits of his money, power, and influence that will, in turn, create opportunities for her to demonstrate and exude her femininity and inspiration.

As men and women are disappointed with their relationship outcomes, each has to ask themselves, what type of man/woman do I qualify for? While you may have been on the dating scene, believing all men are trash or struggling to find the perfect mate, the bottom line is it may very well have been you that has been holding yourself from achieving the happiness you desire. However, it is important to remember that you should stay in your lane in terms

Of what you qualify for. If you struggle to vet the right type of man for you, be sure to seek the guidance and counseling of a qualified therapist. Be sure to identify those qualities you have and how you can change to achieve the relationship outcomes you desire.

GLENN SANDIFER II

CLOSING STATEMENTS

IN *THE MODERN GROUND: HOW TO GET GREAT DATING OUTCOMES IN A MODERN WORLD*, WE HAVE IDENTIFIED HOW WE GOT HERE, WHO MEN ARE, AND WHO WOMEN ARE. HOPEFULLY, YOU SEEK OPPORTUNITIES

TO CONNECT WITH OTHERS AROUND THE CONTENT. HAVE A DIALOGUE WITH YOUR BEST FRIEND, COLLEGE ROOMMATE, OR EVEN - DARE I SAY - PARENT! PART 2 IS AVAILABLE TODAY! THIS DEALS WITH MORE OF THE HARD WORK ON HOW TO GET THE GREAT DATING OUTCOMES. YOU NOW KNOW WHO YOU ARE! IF YOU DON'T LIKE THE TRUTH, BE WILLING TO DO TO THE WORK TO MAKE THE CHANGE. I LOOK FORWARD TO YOU DOING THE WORK NECESSARY TO GET THE OUTCOMES YOU DESIRE!

www.ingramcontent.com/pod-product-compliance
Lightning Source LLC
LaVergne TN
LVHW052003060526
838201LV00059B/3818